1 MONTH OF
FREE
READING

at
www.ForgottenBooks.com

By purchasing this book you are eligible for one month membership to ForgottenBooks.com, giving you unlimited access to our entire collection of over 1,000,000 titles via our web site and mobile apps.

To claim your free month visit:
www.forgottenbooks.com/free909648

ISBN 978-0-266-91876-9
PIBN 10909648

SILVICULTURAL PRACTICES FOR LODGEPOLE PINE IN MONTANA

by

Russell K. LeBarron

- Northern -
Rocky Mountain
Forest & Range
Experiment Station

Missoula Montana

George M. Jemison, Director

UNITED STATES DEPARTMENT OF AGRICULTURE

FOREST SERVICE

TATION PAPER NO 33   JULY 1952

Prepared in the Division of Forest Management Research

FOREWORD

Six years ago, shortly after extensive cutting of lodgepole pine for pulpwood began in Montana, the Experiment Station at the request of Forest Service timber managers, conducted a survey of old and new cuttings in lodgepole pine forests and reviewed publications on the subject of lodgepole pine silviculture. Findings from the study were released in a 15-page mimeographed report entitled "Discussion of Lodgepole Pine Cutting Methods", dated May 21, 1947. It summarized and interpreted past experience in harvesting lodgepole pine, both here and elsewhere; and on the basis of the findings, it also recommended regeneration and cutting practices to be applied in the Continental Divide section of Montana. Five years have elapsed since the report was first circulated, and it has been read widely. During that period, considerable experience has been gained in the Northern Region in harvesting lodgepole pine, particularly for pulpwood.

In looking back to the 1947 report, not many of the comments and recommendations seem to be substantially in error. However, in the light of five years' additional experience, some things can now be said with greater assurance, and a certain amount of amplifying and restating for clarification is needed. In addition, data which pertain to a number of important points have been gathered. This paper brings together the latest information we have in lodgepole pine silviculture.

GEORGE M. JEMISON, DIRECTOR
NORTHERN ROCKY MOUNTAIN FOREST
AND RANGE EXPERIMENT STATION

TABLE OF CONTENTS

A Montana barn, corral and jackleg
fence, made from lodgepole pine

SILVICULTURAL PRACTICES FOR LODGEPOLE PINE IN MONTANA

By

Russell K. LeBarron

"Marking rules for lodgepole pine cover many conditions,
with the supposition that practical application will be
applied in the field." (From a memorandum by Wm. W. Larsen,
Gallatin National Forest, 1/23/30.)

INTRODUCTION

The pioneer miners, railroad builders, and ranchers, who entered Montana
between 1860 and 1880, relied heavily upon lodgepole pine (Pinus contorta)
as a prime source of wood for their occupational requirements. The rail-
roads consumed literally millions of hewn lodgepole pine cross ties. The
miners used immense quantities for stulls, lagging, and charcoal. The
ranchers built thousands of miles of corrals and jackleg fences from this
same tree that the Indians had found so well suited to tepee construction
that it has been named "lodgepole pine". Cutting continued at a high
though probably diminishing rate until about 1930. It should not be for-
gotten that at one time the Deerlodge National Forest ranked first in
volume of cut and stumpage receipts among the national forests of the
Northern Region. Then a variety of economic factors caused the substitu-
tion of other woods and other materials for lodgepole pine in Montana;
and cutting, except for strictly local consumption, almost ceased.

About 1945, lodgepole pine again rather abruptly was brought back into
the timber market. This time the chief bulk product is pulpwood for
high-grade paper pulp, and the highest stumpage value product is transmission line poles. Furthermore, lodgepole pine is increasing in impor-
tance as a lumber species. Today, it seems to be assured of permanent
markets for several important primary products.

Average annual cut of lodgepole pine
from central Montana national forests

Period (Fiscal Years)	Million board feet
1943-45	6
1946-48	23
1949-51	36
1952	52

Pressures to harvest lodgepole pine have required forest managers to improvise rules of cutting because experimental evidence upon which to base sound methods has been lacking. However, Montana's lodgepole pine forests should not be looked upon as virgin timber with which man has had no experience. Many of the timber stands which are being harvested today were cut selectively for some other product 50 years or longer ago.

* * * * * *

Harvesting lodgepole pine with trams and flume. Deerlodge National Forest, about 1912.

* * * * * *

Some of the stands which are now being eyed by pulp-wood operators are growing on land which was cleared by charcoal makers 70 to 80 years ago or which was burned by fires that early settlers witnessed. The harvesting and regeneration problems that confront forest managers today arise from changed logging methods, changed markets, and increasing awareness of the need to protect watersheds and to harvest forests in a planwise way and regenerate them promptly.

GEOGRAPHIC APPLICABILITY

The ideas that will be expressed and the recommendations that will be offered have been developed chiefly from study of lodgepole pine forests growing in mountainous terrain at relatively high elevations where the species often is associated with alpine fir, Douglas-fir and spruce. Most attention has been focused upon central Montana and the part near the Continental Divide. However, the same forest associations occur in many places westward into north Idaho and eastern Washington. Where the climate and topography appear to be similar, the same recommendations probably can be safely applied. On the other hand, where lodgepole pine has invaded the white pine and Douglas-fir zones in north Idaho and northeast Washington, and where it has become established at relatively low elevations, such as the district north of Spokane, Washington, the problems are different, and different silvicultural practices probably are needed.

GENERAL MANAGEMENT CONSIDERATIONS

Before introducing the specific silvicultural and closely related watershed management problems that pertain to keeping the forests productive,
a number of general forest management problems should be considered.
These general management considerations include silvicultural principles,
objectives of management, and potential utilization standards. They are
important because they strongly influence the selection of silvicultural
practices.

First, it is recognized that lodgepole pine is a shade-intolerant species
and should generally be managed as even-aged forest. Silvicultural practices should work toward the purpose of ultimately establishing even-aged
reproduction.

Second, the suggested silvicultural practices are not intended as permanent or final systems. They are intended to aid in converting unmanaged
forests to more uniform and desirable conditions of stocking, thrift, and
age. In some stands, a single harvesting operation may accomplish the
entire process; in others, the adjustment may require a complete rotation
or an even longer period.

Third, a primary objective of forest management is to attain a distribution of age-classes and a degree of stocking that will permit sustained
cutting at a high level. We are reasonably certain that a good many
overmature stands should be held for rather extended periods in order
to level out the age-class distribution and provide a stable base for
the industries that will be consuming the timber. As long as we possess
substantial acreages of overmature timber, the risk of serious losses from
insects, fire, wind, and other destructive agents exists. Therefore, good
judgment is demanded of the timber managers to cut the higher risk timber
first, and flexibility in timber disposal programs is needed.

Reserving the more vigorous or lower-risk timber does not necessarily mean
marking by any particular rule. For example, clear cutting in blocks or
strips can be a very good system for taking out the higher risk timber; so
can partial cutting. But either method can also result in high grading, or
in leaving timber that is exposed to serious danger from wind or other injurious agents.

Fourth, cutting for special products has been the rule rather than the ex-
ception in lodgepole pine forests. Harvesting certain materials such as
pulpwood, charcoal, and lagging results in practical clear cutting. Often,
however, cutting for special products is "selective" but it is not the
selection system of silviculture. Liquidation of special grades of trees
when a good market appears is good business, and it need not be inconsist-
ent with good silviculture, provided the stands are not too heavily thinned
in advance of the final harvest. If properly handled, it may be regarded
as "installment clear cutting".

Little progress has been made in determining what specific protective measures should govern logging lodgepole pine in high-value watersheds. However, confidence in current logging and slash disposal methods has justifiably increased somewhat. We have looked at the cut-overs that have been created during the past six years and while we see some mistakes, they are kinds that can be prevented in future operations. The more tangible and less debatable faults have been concerned with road construction and road maintenance.

From the standpoint of water resource management, cutting in blocks or strips offers distinct advantages. Any kind of a patch-wise cutting system assures that considerable portions of a drainage will be left wholly undisturbed during the period while the cut-over tracts are experiencing the consequences of logging. Cut-over land has somewhat different water run-off characteristics from those of fully-timbered land. Cleared tracts, of course, tend to yield more water and produce peak runoffs earlier during the snow melt period. Hence, a drainage composed partly of uncut timber and partly of deforested land should produce two smaller crests or peak spring flows instead of one larger crest which would occur if the land were either wholly forested or wholly denuded.

Rehabilitation of the timber cover and other corrective measures which may prove to be needed can be effectively scheduled with patch cutting systems before the entire watershed is cut over. In other words, patch cutting is a conservative method that does not stake everything on one throw. It also limits the cumulative effects that may arise from uniform treatment of a large area. For instance, the erosion and other destructive effects of surface water flow increase by a geometric relationship to the quantity of water. Doubling the quantity of water more than doubles its erosive power. Consequently, block cutting reduces maximum effects, whether they be rate of snow melt, gullying, siltation, or peak flows.

The optimum size of clear-cut blocks has been discussed extensively without reaching final conclusions because proof based on experiments is inadequate. Yet experience and logic can point to some definite facts. Small openings in a forest act as snow traps in which snow accumulates and in which melting is retarded by shade from neighboring trees. This so-called "cookie cutter" pattern will give maximum snow storage and maximum retardation of melt. However, since trees do not cast much shade laterally for distances greater than their heights, openings that would offer these advantages would necessarily be extremely limited in size. As a result, the "cookie cutter" type of clear cutting has not received much consideration and has not been tested in Montana. Silviculturally and administratively it has drawbacks, somewhat the same as partial cuttings.

Block clear cuttings from 20 to 75 acres have been most commonly used in Montana. In the original thinking, 20-acre units were suggested because they appeared to be about the size which should be served by a single landing or loading point. In other words, about 20 acres seemed to be a natural logging unit. However, field officers generally reacted unfavorably to the suggested small size and most subsequent discussion has dealt with sizes from 30 or 40 acres up to 75 acres. Currently, clear cut blocks on Forest Service s ales are limited to a maximum size of 50 acres.

In relation to snow storage and melt characteristics, probably only small differences exist between 20-acre and 75-acre blocks, if the same total acreages are logged in a drainage. Twenty-acre units are sufficiently large to lose much of the peculiar advantages of "cookie cutter" openings. Seventy-five-acre units are sufficiently small to preserve a condition of alternating natural forest cover and cut-over land. Both patterns of large and small cutting units require about the same mileage of logging roads and skid trails for a given volume of timber cut. Soil compaction, surface disturbance, and the ease with which water infiltrates the soil should be affected to about the same extent under both systems. The larger size cuttings, of course, permit substantially greater on-site concentrations of the effects.

Strip cutting occasionally is advocated as an alternative to block cutting. Since the two methods are much alike, few convincing points of superiority can be offered for either. Block cutting appears to have, on the average, greater flexibility for adaption to topography and forest conditions.

In addition to destroying, displacing or stirring the litter and organic soil layers, logging and slash disposal considerably affect the permeability of the soil to water. The reaction seems to result chiefly from compaction caused by machinery and logs. In tests in recent clear cuttings the time required for one inch of water to disappear from a five-inch tube set into the soil was measured. Infiltration time was much longer both on skid trails and on some portions of the scarified ground surface where a crawler tractor with a toothed clearing blade had been employed to bunch the slash. The following data show the time for one inch of water to disappear from the five-inch tube:

Ground surface	Soil texture		
	Silt clay loam	Gravelly clay	Stony clay
	(minutes)	(minutes)	(minutes)
Natural surface, cut-over	1.7	4.3	4.0
Burned	2.4	3.4	2.9
Skid trail	28.8	76.6	89.4
Scarified	4.5	54.0	61.9
Uncut forest	4.0	7.5	4.6

Each time statistic in the above tabulation is the average of five or more independent measurements. The longer times required for penetration of water on skid trails show the results of repeatedly compressing the soil with heavy tractors and their loads of logs. In comparison, infiltration rates on the scarified ground were distinctly variable. Evidently the tractor treads had severely compacted the soil on some of the spots that were tested but other spots had been missed by the treads.

The differences in permeability of the various kinds of ground surfaces, as measured by absorption of water from a five-inch tube cannot be directly evaluated. No means is known for determining exactly what are the results in terms of surface water flow, erosion and rate of runoff. Yet, no one can deny that changes in runoff will result and that the reactions will be more or less undesirable. The conclusion seems inescapable, that parts of a watershed should be left undisturbed while the cut-over portions are recovering.

SILVICULTURAL PROBLEMS

RESPONSE TO PARTIAL CUTTING

Overmature lodgepole pine usually is not adapted to partial cutting as a means for arresting stand deterioration or inducing accelerated growth in reserve trees. A permanent sample plot in a tie cutting on the West Yellowstone District, Gallatin National Forest, illustrates how one stand deteriorated after a selective cutting[1]. At the time of cutting in 1926, it was supposed that the residual trees would continue to grow and become ready for harvesting at a later date. A one-half-acre plot was installed to check growth and mortality. The residual trees on the plot were about 170 years of age in 1926, and their diameters ranged from 7.0 to 12.3 inches. Twenty-five years later, only 16 of the original 42 trees remained alive and the average d.b.h. of these survivors had increased only 0.9 inch--approximately 50 annual rings per inch of wood. The cordwood volume of the live trees after 25 years was 52 percent less than the residual volume present when the plot was established. Most of the surviving trees appear likely to die during the next 15 years.

Damage caused by logging machinery has increased the difficulties of encouraging positive net growth by selective cutting. In 1947, ten 1/10-acre plots were established in an overmature stand on the Gallatin National Forest which had been marked for a pulpwood selective cutting. Trees that appeared sufficiently thrifty to warrant reserving them, and trees that were of the size and quality for transmission line poles were marked to leave.

---

[1] Information supplied by Frank B. Casler, Gallatin National Forest.

The pulpwood timber was felled with power saws and skidded in tree
lengths with tractor-drawn arches. A tabulation of the injuries to
trees over 5.5 inches d.b.h. is shown below:

	Trees per acre (Number)
Original stand	191
Marked for reserve	72
Fatal logging damage to reserve trees	22
Non-fatal logging damage to reserve trees	36

Damage probably was unnecessarily high, but the example illustrates the
problem that highly mechanized logging has created.

The foregoing evidence against partial cutting as a means for inducing
net growth should not lead to a sweeping conclusion that selective cutting or other types of partial cutting are always bad. Numerous instances have been observed where individual trees have accelerated their
growth impressively after release. Some stands will continue to gain in
volume for a good many years. Managers should not hesitate to prescribe
selective cutting when the vigor of the trees and other conditions such
as accessibility and market opportunities appear to justify it.

ARRANGEMENT AND SIZE OF BLOCK CLEAR CUTTINGS

Block clear cutting has been recommended partly as a conservative measure for watershed protection. It also creates conditions favorable to
silvicultural management and control of dwarf mistletoe, it encourages
even-aged reproduction, and it breaks up slash areas with intervening
bodies of green timber. As has been pointed out, the size of the blocks
within the range 20 to 75 acres is not too important. The primary considerations that should govern both size and arrangement are:

(1) Condition of the timber. Less thrifty timber should be cut first.
    Although when viewed from a distance, many stands appear to be
    uniform in density, tree size, and other conditions, closer exam-
    ination usually reveals that they are decidedly patchy.

(2) Exposure hazards along the edges of the blocks. To the greatest
    extent possible, the alternating blocks should be arranged to
    minimize wind and other exposure hazards to the reserve blocks.
    For example, good places to put cutting boundaries are borders
    of natural openings, breaks between age classes, ridges, and
    along old roads.

(3) Road locations and logging problems. The blocks, both the cut
    and the reserve, should fit into an orderly logging plan and a
    logical, efficient road system. The boundaries should not create
    "long corners" that will be expensive or impractical to reach,
    either in the first cut or the final operation.

In some places, uniformity of topography and timber types may be such
that a strictly geometric pattern is possible and desirable.

All things considered, 50-acre blocks appear to be large enough for practical purposes in most instances. It is not believed that many situations
will be found where larger units are needed to conform with the guides
that have been recommended for choosing size and arrangement. More places
will be found where the blocks should be substantially less than 50 acres.

REGENERATION

Prompt restocking to the right density with the most desirable species
is at least as important a management objective as harvesting the original timber stand. Lodgepole pine reproduces more promptly and more
abundantly than any other western conifer, which greatly simplifies the
job of foresters. Despite extensive unregulated cutting and uncontrolled
fires during the early days of mining and settlement, comparatively little lodgepole pine land is now in a deforested condition.

Some lodgepole pine regeneration problems are unusual. For instance,
many young lodgepole pine stands become too dense. The writer once
counted 765 ten- to eleven-year-old seedlings on one milacre quadrat in
a burn. The seedlings ranged in height from 4 to 25 inches. Overstocking
causes reduced growth, lengthened economic rotations, and smaller ulti-
mate tree sizes, unless the trees are thinned while still young and small.
Thinning in juvenile stands is a deadweight expense that should be avoided,
if possible.

In a seedbed preparation and slash disposal experiment which is now in
progress near White Sulphur Springs, Montana, four different kinds of
seedbeds--natural forest floor, skidroads, bulldozer scarified ground,
and lopped-scattered slash--bore averages of 6,900 to 8,800 seedlings per
acre two years after slash disposal[2]. With high averages such as these,
some portions of the seedbeds must be even more densely stocked. Some
of the seedlings probably will die but if substantial majorities survive
for ten years or longer, parts of the new stand will be seriously overstocked.

Not all seedbeds in the White Sulphur Springs study exhibited the tendency toward overstocking. The seedbeds where slash had been burned and
where naturally concentrated accumulations of logging slash were left un-
burned are considerably understocked, and are expected to remain that way
until after the new growth becomes old enough to bear seed. For example,
at two years, the spots where natural logging slash concentrations were
burned contained 725 seedlings per acre. A stand density of 725 per acre
would be reasonably satisfactory if the trees were well distributed, but
unfortunately seedlings were present on only 18 percent of the milacre
sampling units. In other words, distribution was decidedly spotty. It
has been said that milacre stocking is a more critical measure than abso-
lute numbers of seedlings per acre, and 65 to 75 percent milacre stocking
has been suggested to be about the optimum[3].

---

[2] Effects of slash disposal on lodgepole pine reproduction. Kenneth N. Boe.
Paper presented at 12th annual meeting of the Montana Academy of Sciences,
Bozeman, Montana, April 12, 1952.
[3] Kenneth N. Boe, cited in Footnote 2.

From the White Sulphur Springs study and other observations of older
cuttings, it can be concluded that most seedbed surfaces will become
amply restocked provided the seed is neither buried in the slash nor
burned. Therefore, special seedbed preparation ordinarily will not be
needed except as it occurs incidentally to slash disposal. More will
be said about the influence of slash disposal in the section on slash.

Lodgepole often regenerates readily under light to moderate timber
cover. In the absence of seed sources of more shade-tolerant tree
species, lodgepole pine forests often develop a distinctly uneven-
aged condition. Yellowstone National Park contains good examples.
The ability to regenerate under conditions somewhat like those in a
shelterwood has led to the establishment of reproduction under old
selective cuttings for ties, lath bolts, converter poles, house logs,
and stulls. In some instances the reproduction is too dense and uniform in size. In other cases, it is comparatively sparse and variable
in uniformity of development.

In Montana, dwarf mis-
tletoe parasitizes all
sizes of lodgepole
pine, but its spread
is most critical dur-
ing the period of

```
***********************
*  This stand was     *
*  cut selectively    *
*  for lath bolts     *
*  25 years earli-    *
*  er.  Note heavy    *
*  witches' brooms    *
*  on residual trees. *
*  Lewis and Clark    *
*  National Forest    *
***********************
```

stand regeneration.
Some regeneration meth-
ods have potentialities
for intensifying the
disease and, in con-
trast, some methods
can be the means for
largely eliminating it.
In open-grown trees,
the parasite often
causes such serious
deformation that the
trees are almost worth-
less. In denser timber

-9-

substantial injury usually is not very apparent until the trees become mature when they often die back from the top and eventually succumb. Thinning the timber seems to accelerate the injurious effects. Brooming becomes more evident and top die-back appears to accelerate. Dwarf mistletoe is not a fast acting lethal organism that must be eliminated as an essential step in management, but its reduction will aid in producing more and better quality products. The key to preventing transmission of dwarf mistletoe from the old stand to the new stand is separation of the two generations of trees. If trees from the old stand are retained during the regeneration period, they are likely to shower mistletoe seed upon the young trees. That has happened in the past whenever stands have been thinned by fire, bark beetle epidemics, and logging.

If reproduction should fail after clear cutting, lodgepole pine can be artificially regenerated either by seeding or planting. A recent seeding and planting test on the Lewis and Clark National Forest resulted in satisfactory establishment both by seed spotting and planting nursery grown trees on a broadcast burned clear cutting[4]. Sod cover, of course, would make initial establishment more difficult and an abnormally dry season might largely eliminate newly planted seeds or seedlings. Nursery propagated trees can withstand drought and vegetative competition better than can seedlings from planted seeds, and nursery stock does not run the risk of destruction by rodents and seed-eating birds.

The steeper south and west slopes which fail to reproduce naturally after a reasonable waiting period can best be regenerated by planting. Scarification to induce natural regeneration would not be advisable on steep ground, nor would it be adequate to counterbalance the unfavorable temperature and moisture conditions on such slopes. South slopes should be looked at critically from the standpoint of whether the sites justify tree planting for timber or watershed management.

Meadows that support vigorous sod-forming grasses are apt to be difficult to reforest. Furthermore, a heavy sod cover assures soil protection and has value for forage. In any particular area, the decision whether or not to attempt reforestation will depend on a number of considerations:

(1) Suitability of habitat for lodgepole pine or other trees. Certain bottom lands and outwash fans at the mouths of ravines are not well adapted to vigorous growth by trees as can be readily judged from existing trees.

(2) Comparative benefits from alternative opportunities to employ the same money.

---

[4] Roe, Arthur L. and Boe, Kenneth N. Spot seeding on a broadcast burned lodgepole pine clear cutting. Northern Rocky Mountain Forest and Range Experiment Station Research Note No. 108. April 1952.

planting or seeding.

STAND IMPROVEMENT

The lodgepole pine type possesses opportunities for comparatively few kinds of stand improvement because it does not contain strikingly inferior competing tree species such as the scrub oaks which are associated with hard pines in the South. Furthermore, the chief products which lodgepole pine is expected to grow--pulpwood, mine stulls, small logs, and poles--cannot be expected to pay back as generously on investments in pruning and other intensive stand improvement operations as do species such as white pine and ponderosa pine on better land. However, at the time of harvesting or within a few years afterwards, many stands can be benefited at relatively low cost by certain silvicultural operations. These include control of dwarf mistletoe and control of stand density. Control of species composition may also be desirable in some places.

Destruction of cull lodgepole pine trees in clear cuttings to prevent carryover of dwarf mistletoe is the most desirable of the stand improvement measures. Probably the cheapest method is to push the culls over with a dozer slash piler if one is being employed for slash disposal. Since dozer piling of the culls along with the slash makes it possible to burn them and eliminates the fire hazard at little extra cost, it generally is the best method. Cull trees also can be girdled, felled, or poisoned with dry Ammate crystals placed in chopped cups. The comparative costs of the latter three methods will depend upon the size of the trees, the skill of the workers, and the equipment. In an experiment in which cull lodgepole pine trees from about 6 to 20 inches d.b.h. were killed, 62 by notch girdling with axes and 44 by placing dry Ammate crystals in chopped cups, both methods required the same time--three to four minutes per tree, including walking time between trees. Notch girdling is not advocated for trees in the size range mentioned because of the tendency to break at the point where girdled. Bark peeling with an axe or one of the special girdling tools can eliminate this disadvantage and speed up the work. Girdling by any method is somewhat objectionable because bark beetles may invade the girdled trees and multiply. Poisoned trees apparently are much less receptive to bark beetle invasion.

Trees up to 3 or 4 inches d.b.h. can be destroyed more efficiently by felling with an axe than by poisoning or axe-girdling. Felling larger trees with a small power saw may prove to be fast, simple, and comparatively low in cost.

Destruction of seedling lodgepole pine advance reproduction to control mistletoe probably is not feasible unless it can be killed more or less incidentally while performing some other task. For instance, reproduction could be at least partially eliminated at no extra cost by putting slash piles on the young trees. They could also be rooted out by dozer pilers in the slash bunching operation.

Establishment of desirable stand density early in life will do much to insure vigorous growth and high yields. Understocked stands can be increased in density by planting or other measures as mentioned in the section on regeneration. Methods for reducing the density of overstocked reproduction are not so well understood. Non-commercial thinning by hand methods is entirely too costly in comparison with the expected gains. Perhaps seedling and small sapling stands where heights do not exceed 25 feet can be thinned rather crudely but effectively and cheaply by dozers or other mechanical equipment. Pilot-plant scale trials are needed to learn more about the methods and results.

Sapling stands which bear serious numbers of Cronartium stem cankers, but are otherwise thrifty would benefit from a sanitation cutting to eliminate infected trees. Stem cankers cause severe cull in many timber products and completely disqualify affected boles for transmission line poles. Sanitation cutting should be limited to rather open-grown or not badly crowded stands, and further, it should be restricted to trees in the upper crown classes which will not be overtopped and suppressed before maturity. These limitations will hold down the cost and insure the largest return in proportion to the investment.

Not infrequently, overmature lodgepole pine stands contain advance growth of alpine fir, spruce, and Douglas-fir. Should advance growth of the more shade-tolerant species be regarded as undesirable? Should the advance growth be eliminated? Categorical answers cannot be given. A thrifty young stand of alpine fir probably will produce as much and as good or better pulpwood than lodgepole pine. Unthrifty alpine fir containing heart rot is almost valueless. Spruce will produce good pulpwood as well as sawtimber. Rocky Mountain Douglas-fir locally is valued more than lodgepole pine for sawtimber. Probably in the majority of instances, the natural conversion to different tree species should not be resisted. However, if the advance growth is poor in quality because of unfavorable site or prolonged suppression, removal to make way for another crop of lodgepole pine would be desirable.

SLASH DISPOSAL

Clear cutting lodgepole pine creates what forest fire authorities regard as serious fuel hazards. In the Northern Rocky Mountain fuel classification system, lodgepole slash is often ranked High (H) in rate of spread and Medium (M) in resistance to control[5].

---

[5] The following terms and code designations indicate comparative rate of spread and resistance to control: Low (L), Medium (M), High (H), and Extreme (E).

In the White Sulphur Springs studies of regeneration and slash disposal little decline in the fuel hazard of logging slash has been observed during the first two years. Lopping and scattering did little to lower the initial danger. On the other hand, both burning out the heavier slash concentrations and dozer piling and burning lowered the fuel ratings immediately. The fuel rating of specially prepared plots in lodgepole pine clear cutting nine months after slash disposal and about one year after logging is shown below[6].

Slash disposal method	Northerly aspects	Southerly aspects
None	H - M	H - M
Lop and scatter	H - M	H - M
Dozer pile and burn	M - M to L - L	M - L to L - L
Broadcast burn	M - M to L - L	L - L

Both broadcast burning and dozer piling and burning meet the Forest Service protection objective, which for cut-over land is L-M or M-L. But their influence on natural regeneration differs significantly. Burning the slash destroys the seed and since broadcast burning covers a larger percentage of the ground surface, it is relatively more destructive by eliminating much of the potential natural regeneration. On the average, broadcast burning covered 44 percent of the sample areas and fires from dozer piles covered only 20 percent. The average net stocking two years after slash disposal by four methods is shown below:[7]

Slash disposal method	Seedlings per acre[8] (Number)	Stocked milacre quadrats per acre (Percent)
None	5,576	63
Lop and scatter	8,833	76
Dozer pile and burn	6,381	65
Broadcast burn	4,340	51

---

[6] Each of the ratings in the tabulation is based upon 3 two-acre samples. Where there was substantial variation in ratings among the 3 replications of each method, the highest and lowest ratings are shown. Prior to slash disposal, almost all plots were rated H - M; a few H - H. The fuel ratings on the plots were classified by Ralph Hand, U. S. Forest Service.

[7] Kenneth N. Boe, cited in Footnote 2, page 8.

[8] Seedling numbers are averages for whole plots including the correct shares of the several kinds of seedbed that result from logging and the named slash disposal method. For example, broadcast burn is composed of 44 percent actual burn stocked at the rate of 725 seedlings per acre, 47 percent natural forest floor with 6,955 seedlings per acre, and 9 percent skidroads with 8,360 seedlings per acre. The net result is 4,340 seedlings per acre.

The comparatively poor distribution of seedlings on the broadcast burned
plots results from the burning of seed on more of the ground surface. If
burning can be limited to a smaller part of the ground, the method probably will give reasonably satisfactory stocking. On the other hand, dozer
piling is more costly but easier to manage and more reliable in terms of
natural reseeding.

Before and after broadcast burning slash in a lodgepole pine
clear cutting. In this instance, the fire covered 87 percent
of the ground surface and hence greatly reduced the potential
natural reseeding. Fuel hazard before burning, High - Medium;
After burning, Low - Low. Lewis and Clark National Forest.

RECOMMENDATIONS FOR SILVICULTURAL PRACTICES

The foregoing discussion has presented the problems and reasons that have
led to development of the recommendations for silvicultural practices
that will be offered. These recommendations should be interpreted with
the understanding that "practical application will be applied in the field".

1.0 Objectives

    1.1 To grow essentially even-aged stands of well-formed thrifty
          trees.

    1.2 To create a desirable distribution of age classes.

    1.3 To improve stand vigor in order to cut down possibilities for
          serious damage from insect and disease epidemics.

1.4 To reduce dwarf mistletoe infection.

1.5 To maintain desirable watershed conditions.

1.6 To minimize fire danger and promote economical, effective fire control.

1.7 To harmonize timber use with other forest uses.

2.0 Definitions

2.1 Stocking

2.11 Well stocked. Stands that have generally unbroken canopies which prevent lodgepole pine reproduction from making substantial headway.

2.12 Understocked. Stands that were naturally so lightly stocked and stands that have been thinned enough, as by bark beetles or logging, that lodgepole pine reproduction, shrubs and grasses can grow reasonably well.

2.2 Maturity

2.21 Mature. Stands generally more than 120 to 140 years in age. These ages are believed to correspond with the time when most stands fall off in vigor and net growth declines. Individual trees, of course, vary greatly in the ages when they reach highest economic usefulness and pathological maturity.

2.22 Immature. Stands generally less than 120 to 140 years in age.

2.3 Composition

2.31 Pure stands. More than 90 percent lodgepole pine by volume or number of stems in the overstory.

3.0 Timber marking

3.1 Mature and overmature stands

3.11 Pure lodgepole pine

3.111 Well stocked

3.1111 Clear cut if markets permit utilization of all trees 6 inches d.b.h. and larger. Limit clear cut units to about

-15-

50 acres or less, interspersed with at least equal areas of reserved timber. Use care in selecting boundaries to avoid creating bad risks for wind and other exposure damage. Cut higher risk blocks first and hold intervening blocks at least 20 years until cut-over units have restocked, unless high mortality necessitates cutting sooner.

3.1112 Cut selectively if markets can absorb only certain classes of trees, but limit cutting including logging damage and skid road removals to not more than 25 percent of the stand basal area in order to prevent accelerated stand deterioration and to retard restocking by lodgepole pine until the final harvest cutting.

3.1112 Understocked

3.1121 Even-aged. Cut lightly, heavily, or clear, depending upon the market opportunities and the stand. Watch for chances to reserve trees that will grow to size for higher value products such as transmission line poles by making small increases in diameter--say 1 to 3 inches. Encourage loggers to thin over-dense patches of reproduction while felling and skidding. If advance reproduction of lodgepole pine or other species is well established, no restrictions need be placed on size of clear cuttings.

3.1122 Uneven-aged. Cut selectively, removing, if marketable, all older trees and younger trees that because of spacing, disease, form or lack of vigor, are undesirable to leave for further growth. Mark to reduce mistletoe infection unless it is so prevalent that removal will result in excessively heavy cutting.

3.12 Mixed species composition

3.121 Cut each species according to its requirements. No systematic attempt should be made to discriminate against any commercially useful species that is ecologically well adapted to the habitat.

-16-

3.1211 Spruce grows vigorously to much greater
ages than lodgepole pine. In creek
bottoms, it can be held to sizes of
about 24 inches, and on slopes to about
16 inches. Stands in which spruce is
reserved should not be thinned more
than 25 percent by volume.

3.1212 Alpine fir in mixture with lodgepole pine
should be cut heavily because it is apt
to deteriorate from heart rot while still
small. Make a preliminary check to deter-
mine prevalence of heart rot as an indi-
cation of the suitability of the site for
production of alpine fir. Encourage loggers to thin dense thickets of alpine fir
advance reproduction.

3.1213 Thrifty Douglas-fir trees in mixture with
lodgepole pine are good to leave for
growth to large sizes (24 to 30 inches
d.b.h.) unless they are exceptionally
bad in form or limbiness.

3.2 Immature stands. Currently the main lodgepole pine management
problems are concerned with protecting, harvesting, and re-
generating overmature timber. Therefore, cutting in immature
stands should generally be deferred. As a general guide, improvement cuttings in immature stands are recommended wherever
enough well-formed, thrifty trees can be reserved to mature in
a well-stocked condition at age 120 to 140 years. Watch particularly to take out trees bearing Cronartium stem cankers or
dwarf mistletoe. In 80-year-old stands, reduce basal area to
not less than 80 square feet per acre, and in 100-year-old
stands to not less than 105 square feet.

4.0 Slash disposal

4.1 Clear cut areas. In general, limit destruction of slash by
burning to what is required to meet forest protection standards. Dozer slash pilers should be employed for concentrat-
ing slash in preparation for burning unless steep slopes or
heavy jackpots of dead and down timber make the method difficult and inefficient. Spot burn jackpots and naturally concentrated slash, especially if the fires can be prevented
from spreading over more than about 25 percent of the ground.
Eliminate all slash immediately adjacent to blocks of green
timber. Lopping and scattering is not recommended. The
merits of supplemental special protection in lieu of slash
elimination should be considered in some instances.

4.2 Partially cut areas. Pile and burn slash to the extent required by forest protection standards. Felling trees away from roads, other hazardous areas, and streams will help prevent the accumulation of slash in places where it is particularly undesirable and costly to eliminate.

4.3 Commercial improvement cuttings in young stands. No slash disposal.

5.0 Stand improvement

5.1 Kill or destroy cull dwarf mistletoe-infected trees over about 3 inches d.b.h. in clear cuttings. Employ dozer slash pilers or hand methods including poisoning, girdling, or felling, whichever method is cheaper or better.

5.2 Plant clear cut creek bottoms which do not regenerate within 3 years. Lodgepole pine, spruce, and Douglas-fir should be considered. Base choice of species mainly on suitability to the habitat.

5.3 Plant other cut-over tracts where natural reproduction has failed, about three years after cutting, if justified for watershed protection or timber production. As a guide for fill-in planting, (a) plant no trees or seed spots less than 10 feet from naturally established seedlings and (b) plant no trees unless at least 16 can be planted in a continuous line or blocks, spaced 7 x 7 feet. In other words, a non-stocked spot should be at least 48 feet square or 20 feet wide and 132 feet long.

5.4 Fell dominant trees infected with Cronartium stem cankers to favor sound competitors in thrifty sapling growth.

5.5 Thin with bulldozers or slash bunchers in dense reproduction less than 25 feet tall, but only on a trial basis or pilot-plant scale until the method and results become better understood.

6.0 Erosion prevention measures

6.1 Locate, construct, and maintain logging roads and main skid trails to specifications that either eliminate concentration of surface water, or provide for prompt dispersal before it can cause damage.

6.2 Make more skid trails and use them lightly where the topography and skidding methods permit. Skid trails that are used repeatedly which run diagonally across a slope collect more water than lightly used skid trails or skid trails that run straight down the slope.

6.3 Construct water diversions from skid trails promptly after completion of logging.

6.4 Work heavy slash into the skid roads and landings where possible, during skidding or machine slash disposal. Few instances have been observed where slash scattered by hand methods on skid roads has prevented surface water flow or caused diversion of the water.